Coach Them Well

Coach Them Well

FOSTERING FAITH & DEVELOPING CHARACTER IN ATHLETES

Dale D. Brown
David Cutcliffe
Kelly Herrmann
Timothy F. Welsh

Saint Mary's Press®

Genuine recycled paper with 10% post-consumer waste. 5116400

The publishing team included Steven C. McGlaun, development editor; Lorraine Kilmartin, reviewer; Mary Koehler, permissions editor; prepress and manufacturing coordinated by the prepublication and production services departments of Saint Mary's Press.

Cover photos by Kimberly K. Sonnek

Printed in the United States of America

Printing: 9 8 7 6 5 4 3 2 1

Year: 2014 13 12 11 10 09 08 07 06

ISBN-13: 978-0-88489-933-4
ISBN-10: 0-88489-933-0

Library of Congress Cataloging-in-Publication Data

Coach them well : fostering faith and developing character in athletes
/ Dale D. Brown ... [et al.].
    p. cm.
ISBN-13: 978-0-88489-933-4 (pbk.)
ISBN-10: 0-88489-933-0 (pbk.)
    1. Catholic coaches — United States. 2. Coaching (Athletics) —
Religious aspects — Catholic Church. I. Brown, Dale, 1935- .
BX4669.C63 2006
259.088'796 — dc22

                                                           2005037420

CONTENTS

INTRODUCTION

The Increasing Role of Sports in the Lives of Youth

A recent survey by the National Catholic Education Association (NCEA) discovered that more than 70 percent — almost three out of every four — of Catholic high school students are involved in either interscholastic or intramural sports. This means that almost the same number of youth are in contact with someone they call "coach." More often than not, that coach is an adult who has decided to work with young people in the arena of athletics. Coaches range from the volunteers who spend a few hours a week coaching junior league football to the head coaches or athletic directors at large high schools and at universities. The purpose of *Coach Them Well: Fostering Faith and Developing Character in Athletes* is to acknowledge the role that coaches play in the physical and moral development of young people. Through this resource, we want to extend a partnering hand to all coaches as they help form the faith and character of the athletes under their care. We want to do this by helping coaches understand themselves as people of faith and character.

What's Inside?

No coach is perfect, and that goes for the authors of *Coach Them Well.* These coaches do bring to the table a love of young people, a passion for the sports they coach, a deep faith nurtured by the Catholic Church, and a belief that athletics and faith do not compete with or contradict each other. In fact, the authors believe that athletics can be the gateway to spiritual development and emotional maturity. The coach can be the guide on that journey.

In this book you will find four college coaches' reflections on the ministry of coaching. The reflections contain the coaches' faith stories, as well as the insight gained through more than one hundred years of combined coaching experience. The coaches also share compelling stories about the students they have coached. The four coaches represent the diversity of coaching itself. From the reflections of an NCAA Division I football coach to the thoughts of a Catholic university women's basketball coach, from the reflections of an NCAA Final Four football coach about the hurdles athletes must clear to the thoughts of the Notre Dame University men's swimming coach on the importance of mentoring—*Coach Them Well* presents a wealth of knowledge from the experiences of coaches who have mentored, led, coached, and competed at all levels.

Making the Common Uncommon

A. Bartlett "Bart" Giamatti, the former president of Yale University in New Haven, Connecticut, and current Major League Baseball commissioner, sees sports as an entry point into something larger in the lives of its participants.

> Sport is an instrument for vision, and it ever seeks to make the common—what we all see, if we look—uncommon. Not forever, not impossibly perfect, but uncommon enough to remain a bright spot in the memory, thus creating a reservoir of transformation to which we can return when we are free to do so. (*Take Time for Paradise: Americans and Their Games*, p. 15)

Coaches have the opportunity to make the common uncommon and to transform the lives of young people for the better. As you read these reflections, may you be renewed in your ministry of coaching and inspired to shepherd closer to God the youth in your care.

KELLY HERRMANN

Kelly Herrmann is currently the coordinator of intramural athletics, as well as the women's volleyball and basketball coach, for Franciscan University in Steubenville, Ohio. From 1988 to 1991, Kelly served as the athletic director for Franciscan University. In 1987, Kelly earned her BS degree in education from the university. Kelly has coached at all educational levels, from junior high through college and university. While attending college, she helped coach a local high school team.

Kelly and her husband, John, who is the director of student financial services at Franciscan University, are strongly committed to campus life and the faith formation of the youth they serve. In addition to her coaching and intramural coordinator responsibilities, Kelly serves as an adviser to one of the campus households—small faith communities whose same-gender members meet for support, bonding, and faith formation. Kelly and John strive to help students live healthful, balanced, faith-filled lives.

Kelly and John have six children—Johnny, Peter, Leo, Emily, Kevin, and Michael—whom they home-school. Kelly's commitments as a wife, mother, teacher, coach, and mentor reflect her belief that God calls her and John to live their faith and share it in an evangelistic way with the students at Franciscan University.

CHAPTER 1

Coach as Shaper of Faith Through Athletics

Kelly Herrmann

The Uniqueness of Coaching in a Catholic School

Occasionally, people ask me, "What makes coaching at a Catholic school different from coaching at any other school?" I have generally found the difference, to my great sadness, to be not much. Many coaches seem unable to base their coaching decisions on things that should matter, such as character, faith, integrity, example, and so on. All too often, they make decisions based on wins versus losses. As well as any coach, I understand the pressure to win that exists in the sports world. Regardless of where we coach, the old adage "It's not whether you win or lose, it's how you play the game" simply isn't seen to be true anymore. At all levels of play, the message is to win—at any cost. Even at the youngest ages, the first question children often hear after a game is, Did you win? Yet, other questions demand important answers with long-lasting consequences, such as the following: Did you give 100 percent? Did you work well with your teammates? Did you take the coaches' instructions well? But the pressure to win exists, no matter who you are and regardless of your league.

With a heightened focus on winning in the culture of sports, maybe those of us in Catholic schools should ask a different question: What should be different about coaching in a Catholic school? My experience coaching in public schools, recreational settings, Catholic schools, and now at Franciscan University of Steubenville, Ohio, is that I must live as an example. I must live as though I seriously believe in Jesus Christ. Moreover, I can and should share this belief with my athletes.

Living Your Belief in Jesus Christ

As I mentioned, my first task as a faith-filled coach is to set an example for my athletes, the referees, the spectators, and the peer coaches. The effect coaches can have on their players cannot be overstated. Working together, sweating together, and being committed to common goals as a team powerfully and profoundly bind a team to its coach. In many instances, these bonds can last a lifetime. I have noticed that the greater the sacrifice and commitment, the greater the benefit for all the people on the team — players and coaches.

The coach's job is to teach the X's and O's. The coach can also teach so much more. The players learn from the coach's manner and attitude. If the coach expects the players to be hard workers, the coach must be a hard worker. If the players are to be selfless, the coach must be selfless. In a Catholic school, living and exemplifying a Catholic lifestyle are just as important for the coach as for the players. Coaches can talk about being the best we can be, striving for excellence, reaching our goals, and sacrifice. Yet what better reason is there to take up the task than this: Christ calls us to!

Christ doesn't call us coaches to mediocrity. He calls us to do our best in everything we do. From game planning to managing practice, from administrative tasks to relating with assistants, we act differently from other people because of Christ's call. A Catholic coach living his or her faith, showing the way to players during, and away from, competition, can bring players into a far deeper spiritual experience. A coach who is an expert at the game but who only barks out "Work hard" and "Be committed because I said so" is missing an opportunity to show the way.

As a wife, a mother of six, a coordinator of intramural athletics, and a women's basketball and volleyball coach, I try hard to live my Catholic faith in everything I do. Living as a disciple of Christ is a daunting task at which I daily fall short. But I'm still in the race. I rely on my faith, the sacraments, and my church community for support and guidance. Instead of keeping such support private, I try to model it to the women I coach. I want them to see that, imperfect though I am, my faith and my community of faith are vital to my life as a person and as a coach. I try to affect the lives of the women I coach in a much greater way than merely improving their jump shot. Coaching at a Catholic institution like Franciscan University gives me the opportunity and freedom to live my faith and share it with my players. Do I have to know the game? Absolutely. But knowing and living my faith are equally important.

Setting Goals

I want to win as badly as the coaches against whom I compete. The nature of sports is that there will be winners and there will be losers. Because of this love to compete and win, coaches set familiar goals:

- improve in specific areas, such as rebounding or shooting percentage
- improve our record from the previous year
- beat a specific team
- win our conference title

But beyond the goals that result from being better competitors, the teams I coach also set spiritual goals. These include things like the following:

- pray together
- set aside time for Eucharistic adoration
- pray for one another every day
- learn ways to forgive one another
- be Christ to one another
- encourage one another to seek and live out God's call as a student and athlete

Such goals reflect how much more our experience of participating in sports can be. We want to win. But if the athletes' goals are to learn skills for life, to grow into a community, to become holier people, and to evangelize, then our goals will have an effect beyond the sound of the final horn.

Representing a Catholic School
in the Heat of Competition

There are no assurances that athletes from a Catholic school are always going to represent their school in an exemplary manner. There are no assurances when it comes to any human's behavior. As a team, we try our best, despite the reality that we often fall short.

Sport is a microcosm of the Christian life. We try, we struggle, and we seek forgiveness: from God, our teammates, our opponents, and the officials. We deal with the consequences of our negative behavior as Christians should. We acknowledge what we did and accept the penalty with the attitude of a mature person. Hopefully, we learn life's lessons, and we are better, more mature people for it.

Seeing Faith Development Firsthand

During the first year of our program at Franciscan University, I had a senior on our team whom I will refer to as Karen. I knew Karen well, because she was a part of the household I served as adviser. Households are volunteer student groups focused on Christian support and prayer. Karen was always special to me. Even though we never spent much time together outside the household, Karen obviously loved Jesus and tried to live a committed Christian life. As I got to know Karen a little better, I learned that she was raised in a devoutly Catholic home. Karen seemed to be doing well at Franciscan University and wanted to play basketball.

About six months before the start of our first basketball season, Karen began working at a local pub as a bartender, to earn much-needed income. Over the next few months, Karen really began to struggle. She was having a difficult time sticking to her schedule, and she was struggling in her prayer life. When we talked, I felt that her job was asking her to compromise too much on her schedule, her sleep, and her energy. The worst part was how her work was affecting her spirit.

As we approached the start of the basketball season, all of the young women were excited, but none more so than Karen. She was a true competitor and a gifted athlete, and she played for all the right reasons. Knowing Karen and her strength and spirit, I was cautiously optimistic that she would, with God's help, get her life back on track.

I remember a conversation I had with the university's athletic director before our season tryouts. We were talking about the team, and he was asking who would be the captains and team leaders. When I mentioned Karen's name, he laughed. Now, make no mistake, he knew Karen and really wanted to see her do well, but he had serious questions about her ability to fulfill the duties of a team captain. He said, "If Karen is a reliable leader, I will eat the field house." I told him I believed in her and I thought that the commitment basketball demanded could help her.

Any questions I had were answered the first week of practice. She was there every day, right on time, and when I asked the captains — including Karen — to come to a meeting at 7:00 a.m. before an early Saturday practice, she was there, too — despite having worked until 3:30 early that morning. As the weeks went on, and we got closer to our first game, Karen came into my office and said, "I can't do this anymore." She had come to realize that the bartending job was too much of a drain, too much of a compromise, and that she had to make changes. She scaled back her work schedule to one night a week and eventually just quit the job.

Little by little, she got her schedule under control. She had more time for Mass and prayer. She was working out hard and getting in shape. It was all so positive. We had a successful first season, winning 60 percent of our games and laying the foundation for what has become a very positive program.

Shortly after our season had ended, Karen was at my house. My husband and children had gone to bed, and Karen and I were talking. She said, "Kelly, I think basketball saved my life," and she recounted how badly she had been struggling before that season. As Karen thanked me, I looked back, trying to think of what exactly I had done for her. But it hadn't been me. God had helped her. It brings tears to my eyes to think of how a positive team experience like that can affect athletes in so many different ways, how God uses many avenues to steer his struggling ones back to him.

I know, as a coach, there are many things I do or don't do in particular situations. I have to be demanding in some situations and patient and understanding in others. But as a Catholic coach at a Catholic school, I think the two most important things I do to help my players are to love them and to pray for them. Having six children, I know what a mother's love is. I try to love my players in the same way—not necessarily in an outwardly emotional way, but by being the one to stand behind them, sometimes holding them up, sometimes pushing them forward. Each player needs or allows me to do this in different ways and to different degrees. I trust that God knows what they need, and if it's not help from me, God will send someone else.

Prayer is the most important part of our team life. Not a day goes by that I don't intercede for my players, be it in my family rosary, during night prayers with my children, at Mass, or before the Blessed Sacrament. I grew up as the middle of nine children, and my siblings always tell stories about how I never stopped begging until I got my way. I have heard speakers compare intercession to a child's begging the parents for something and not wanting to take no for an answer. Well, that was me, and I try to have that same persistence now.

Each Athlete Is Unique

I am always overwhelmed by the uniqueness of God's children. I see it in my own children, in how they are similar and yet so different, so complex in their thoughts and feelings and in their responses to challenge and conflict. I see the same thing in my players and the other students at Franciscan University. God created all of us differently, so it pains me to see coaches with a certain coaching style expecting all of their players to fit into that style. I try to get to know players so I can have some insight into what motivates them. What encourages one but at the same time discourages another? Why do some respond well to being confronted with expectations and to feeling the security of the system of which they are a part, while others crumble with just a disapproving word? Some coaches would say, "Get over it." There is certainly a time and a place for mental toughness and for challenging athletes to be able to handle more today than they could yesterday. But we can't lose sight of their differences and how to use those differences to find the balance that makes the athletes fit together as a team.

Each Situation Is Unique

I had a player, whom I will call Michelle, who was on medication for depression. She had been doing well for some time, so when she came down with a stomach virus and wasn't able to take her medication for a few days, she thought maybe she didn't need it. A few mornings later, during a lively scrimmage, she had an altercation with a teammate. After a meeting with the two players, I was left shaking my head, wondering what had happened and why Michelle had responded as she did. Soon, she told me that she hadn't been taking her medication. In a different situation, I would have suspended Michelle for the altercation. To complicate the situation, she was a senior, we were approaching the last weekend of our season, and her parents were flying in from halfway across the country to see her play for the last time ever.

I know that ten or fifteen years earlier, I would have handled the situation differently. I would have seen it as merely black and white, crime and punishment. But that day, I really felt that God gives us far more than one more chance, and I should do the same for Michelle. I think God wanted me to show his mercy, to reach out to the lost sheep. Michelle wasn't someone just making bad choices. Her bad choice was simply not taking her medicine.

We had back-to-back games that weekend, so I suspended Michelle from the first game, asking her to dress in warm-up clothes and cheer for her teammates. It was a difficult time for her, and for me, as well. Some players on the team didn't agree, so they had a difficult time, too. But Michelle sat and cheered for her teammates, did exactly what I asked of her, and went out and played very well that last game in front of her parents.

I think the team learned a lot that weekend. Maybe we won't realize it for years to come, but someday, what we all learned will come to help us. I know Michelle, at the very least, learned something about herself and probably much more.

Accepting Imperfection

I have a senior captain, whom I will call Terri. We call her "the chief." She is a true leader, driven and striving for excellence in everything she does. She maintains a 4.0 grade point average (GPA) in biology, attends daily Mass, and I could go on and on. I quickly learned that Terri's struggle is to accept her best, even if she falls short of perfection, which isn't often. As our starting point guard for three years, Terri has always had to handle pressure. She has never backed down. When Terri has made a mistake, I haven't needed to point it out, show my frustration, or get in her face with a motivational speech to avoid another mistake. She simply says "sorry" and tries to do better. Terri is one of those unique athletes who has all the motivation she needs inside. My job is to keep her positive, help her accept her humanness, and teach her to see that her best—not perfection—is good enough. Our faith tells us to strive to be like Christ but also to know that the perfection of Christ is an unattainable goal. The disappointment we feel when we fall short can be overwhelming. I know Terri has felt that disappointment. I also know that the times she has struggled on the court will help lead her to that point of self-awareness when her best is good enough, when she will feel God's love and see the smile on his face simply because she gave her all.

Meeting Them Where They Are

I once coached another athlete, whom I will call Lisa. She had lost her father at age 12 and really struggled with her self-worth. Lisa was a talented player and an extremely creative, bright person. Unfortunately, her self-esteem was very much tied to her performance as an athlete. Always feeling she had to prove herself, and acting out of her insecurity, she often made herself the center of attention. She was a classic example of someone who seemed confident and secure only because she was so insecure. This was another situation where, ten or fifteen years ago, I would have said, "No. You don't fit here. You take too much time and energy, and the team can't take the risk."

A positive team experience can do so much for an athlete. In Lisa's case, she needed sports and the structure it provided to find herself. Without it, I believe she would have been devastated. I learned much about her over the years. For example, she would only text-message me when asking for help, because she didn't want to be needy or a burden. As long as she always responded appropriately to correction—and she always did—then she had a place on our team. So much grace is poured out on the contrite, on those who admit weakness and sincerely repent.

Over time, Lisa even developed a sense of humor about her struggles. One night, we were cleaning up the gym after a fund-raiser that our team had sponsored. Lisa had gotten the impression that a few players had left early before our cleanup was finished. She went into a mild rant about how terrible it was that they had left early and about what she would have done to punish them if she were the coach. I half-jokingly said, "It's a good thing you aren't the coach, because you would have kicked yourself off the team a long time ago." Everyone burst out laughing, including Lisa. My point was well taken. A few moments later, the two players Lisa believed had left early came walking back into the gym. They had been waiting for a security officer to come and unlock a storage room so they could put away chairs. Retelling the story, we laughed again. That Lisa could laugh at herself told much about the progress in her life and the direction God was leading her.

Moral Issues Athletes Face

Athletes face different moral conflicts at different levels of age, ability, and competition. We hear more and more about major college athletes who are put on such a pedestal that they think they can get away with everything, from accepting illegal gifts from boosters, to performing poorly in the classroom, to getting into trouble with the law. How quickly we can lose sight of who gave us the gifts and talents we have and of their intended purpose—to glorify God.

At Franciscan University, we are a small program, so the moral issues our athletes face are more rooted in the relational issues of working together as part of a team and in the way we live our faith during the heat of battle. Our athletes don't fit academics into a career in sports. Rather, they fit sports into an academic life to prepare them for jobs, marriage, religious life, and countless other issues they will encounter after college. For this reason, the focus for our athletes at Franciscan University is very different from that of "big-time college" sports. Having said that, it is also true that in the heat of battle, our convictions come to the surface. As a coach, I try to set a high standard for my players' behavior. I demand that they maintain their composure and that they act in a way that pleases our Lord, no matter the circumstances. And when they fail—and we all fail sometimes—we recognize our weakness, make amends wherever necessary, and hopefully learn and become better people for it. Sometimes, Christian athletes come under intense scrutiny, as though simply because they believe in and love God, they should never make mistakes, never struggle, or never fall short. Of course, that's not real life. Just because our students have strong convictions doesn't mean they always have the strength and maturity to live out those convictions. Sports are really a microcosm of life. That is what makes them so valuable. We learn so much about ourselves when we are tested, and that self-awareness helps us learn, grow, and handle the next challenge better than the last.

The significance of a team experience cannot be overstated when trying to handle the challenges we face in life. To struggle alongside a teammate or to be committed to other people fosters the ability to rely on others and to be relied upon. That concept of strength in numbers really rings true. Because players are committed to the team and one another, when they say no to something negative and yes to something positive, they speak for the team, and the entire team stands behind them. Saying yes to an early bedtime so they can make a 6:00 a.m. practice, yes to studies to keep their GPA where it needs to be, yes to a positive attitude, because their teammates depend on them—all these things give them the strength to say no to losing their temper on the court, skipping class, abusing alcohol, and the list goes on and on.

Be Christ to One Another

For me, it all begins and ends with my faith and belief in Christ. If our total program is directed toward Christ, and if we strive to live our faith through our sports involvement, and not in spite of it, then we develop the total person. Then the standard is raised not just by the school administration or the coach but also by the players themselves. The players begin to feel the internal drive toward love and commitment for Christ and one another, and their behavior reflects that feeling.

We constantly encourage one another to live our faith, on and off the court. We pray before every game to be Christ to our opponents and to the people who come to watch us play. We invite our opponents to pray with us after every game, taking the opportunity to forgive and seek forgiveness whenever necessary. This tradition is also a part of every intramural game held on campus.

We coaches strive to bring the Gospel into every situation in which we have the opportunity to affect our athletes. Quite simply, the guiding message I hope every athlete I encounter takes from me is the need to be Christ to one another and to see each moment of every day as a chance to glorify God through actions and words. That is what I strive to do with each athlete I am blessed to work with.

DAVID CUTCLIFFE

David Cutcliffe served six years as the head coach at the University of Mississippi—or Ole Miss—located in Oxford, Mississippi, from 1999 to 2004, posting forty-four wins and twenty-nine losses. David was the only coach in school history to win at least seven games in each of his first five seasons. In 2003, he was named the Associated Press Southeastern Conference (SEC) Co-Coach of the Year, as well as being named Coaches SEC Coach of the Year. Over the course of David's time at Ole Miss, his teams recorded one Cotton Bowl victory and three Independence Bowl victories. Before his tenure at Ole Miss, David served for seventeen years on the coaching staff of the University of Tennessee in Knoxville, including six years as the assistant head coach and offensive coordinator.

A native of Birmingham, Alabama, David attended the University of Alabama in Tuscaloosa, after graduating from Birmingham's Banks High School in 1972. Unable to continue his playing career, he was able to work with the Ole Miss football program and staff to help prepare him for his chosen profession of coaching. After receiving his BS degree from Ole Miss in 1976, David's dream of becoming a football coach was quickly realized as he returned to his alma mater, Banks High School, as an assistant coach.

Currently, David resides in Knoxville, Tennessee, with Karen, his wife of twenty-two years, and their three children, Chris, Katie, and Emily. David is extensively involved in the life of his church, as well as in the Fellowship of Christian Athletes (FCA). Additionally, David has a busy schedule of speaking and broadcast engagements.

CHAPTER 2

Being a Coach of Character

David Cutcliffe

The Lessons My Parents Taught Me

My faith story begins early in my childhood. I had parents who understood the importance of raising their children in the Church. We were devout Catholics, and my father made sure we attended Mass wherever we were. My father had been raised Catholic and saw the Church as a major part of his life. My mother had been raised in the Methodist denomination and later converted to Catholicism. She is, to this day, the best practicing Catholic I have ever known. My siblings and I knew from an early age that our parents expected that we would be involved in the life of our church. I fondly recall being dropped off at the church each weekday morning at 6:00 by my father on his way to work, so I could be the altar server at the 6:30 Mass. In the course of this service, I got to know our priest, who was from Ireland, and also grew in my faith through the talks we shared.

Another critical lesson I learned early, but didn't quite understand at the time, was the importance of having my priorities in proper order. My family was not poor by any means, but I was always looking at the way others who were more financially fortunate than we were dressed and carried themselves. Eventually, I understood that my parents sacrificed many things they could have had for themselves to make sure their children were comfortable, well loved, cared for.

For my parents, what was important was presence, not presents. We never went without anything when I was growing up, but we also did not have an abundance of possessions. We did have an abundance of family and faith. For example, even though six children were in our family, my mom did not work outside the home, so she could be there with us. My parents' values were in place, and we were happier for that fact. Today, each day in our lives as parents, my wife and I have striven to have our children grow up with the same experience, so we can return the favor my parents did for me.

Lessons I Learned Away from Home

When I was fifteen, I experienced major losses in my life. Within a short time, both my father and one of my brothers died tragically and unexpectedly. For the first time in my life, my mother had to take a job outside the house. With all of these dramatic changes going on, I needed someone to lean on, and my coaches were there for me. Their support in a difficult time helped model the type of coach I would strive to become.

No one event shaped my life spiritually, but as the years went by, I did find spirituality in my coaching responsibilities. The shaping of young men's lives is such a big responsibility that you have to find strength and wisdom through prayer and God's word. Inviting God into my life as a coach helped me find my own spirituality dealing with my program at Ole Miss, in Oxford, Mississippi. I had to set the tempo of the program. If I were sincere about the role I was inviting God to play in my life and my coaching, I had to acknowledge a responsibility to the kids I coached beyond teaching X's and O's and physical conditioning.

What Does It Mean to Be a Person of Character?

Competition in the true sense of the word is fair. Victory is the reward for discipline and hard work. Fairness means all the competitors have the same opportunity to prepare, to play within the same rules, to have similar equipment, and so on. Athletic competition is one of the last venues of our society where fairness can be expected. In any given competition, on any given day, an underdog can rise up and win. The unexpected can happen, because all the competitors have an equal chance at victory. This also means that in any given competition, things can go wrong, and our team can lose.

Faith is critical to dealing with competition, victory, and defeat. Both victory and defeat are fleeting. They are mere moments in a larger timeline. I coach with the understanding that I cannot control the scoreboard but can control how my team prepares for, accepts, and deals with the consequences of an outcome. It is a commonly used axiom that life is a journey. I have often told my teams and coaches to treat both victory and defeat as imposters, because neither is permanent. Preparing for those moments is important. It is also vital to prepare and focus on the everyday parts of life, to focus on the larger journey.

In coaching, we know that if we are to be viewed as successful, we must win. In striving to win, we might meet countless challenges to our character. At the Division I level, I have found it is easy for us coaches to get caught up in ourselves, our jobs, and our popularity, to the point that they become more important than God and our families. This goes back to one of the early lessons my parents taught me: we must maintain our priorities. Every decision we make is weighted. Each of us decides what is most important to us. In athletics, problems arise when too much importance is placed on the game and on winning. When the game becomes the most important thing in our lives, it becomes easy to ignore things such as family and faith. It also becomes easier to compromise our values and characters to get the win.

Coaches of Character

Character is shown in what we do when we think no one is looking. It is our core. Coaches of character put what is right before what may be popular. Coaches of character lead by more than words. They lead by example in how they live their lives. It is a matter of being consistent. Whether I am on the sideline on national TV or in the privacy of my office, I act and speak the same way. Coaches of character don't change, especially in front of their teams. I have witnessed coaches who in public are proper and respectful, yet when they are alone with their team, they curse and use abusive language. Youth pick up on this hypocrisy and lose respect for those coaches and programs each time it happens.

We have all heard stories of dysfunctional families. There is also such a thing as dysfunctional teams. In a team setting, the dysfunction almost always starts with the coaching staff. If we demand character from our teams, we have to demand it from ourselves. It is not easy to do, and it is difficult to learn. Nobody is perfect. The key is this: each time we make a mistake, we should learn from it and grow. Just as victory is fleeting, so too are failure and mistakes. A mistake is never final unless we allow it to be.

One of the ways the coaches' characters manifest themselves is in how the coaches treat the players on their team. We must treat players with respect. We must treat them as we would our own children. We have to be thorough in all aspects of physical, mental, and spiritual development. When we must discipline, we should do so with respect. It is not easy, but it is essential. I've been angry with an athlete or team before, but being angry and getting our message across without being disrespectful is possible. In Division I football, I have discovered that everyone — the administration, the fans, the boosters, the team, the student body, the parents — is watching each of my actions. My rules for my coaches in terms of disciplining athletes are simple. Do not humiliate. Do not use vulgar language. Do not soft-shoe around the problem. Each situation is unique, and there is rarely an easy solution. I discovered a long time ago that what is right is not always popular with the fans, families, school, media, or team. That is where character comes in. If my decision is grounded in what is best for the players and the team — not necessarily in terms of wins and losses, but in terms of developing young men of character — then I can weather any criticism with my head held high. Putting character first with athletes is a commitment to coaching them all the time, not just on the practice field or game field.

What Is Constant Coaching?

Coaching is teaching, and we never quit coaching. At every moment, we can coach, on and off the field. And we must never pass up an opportunity to coach, be it a blocking assignment or life lesson. I have been fortunate to have more ups than downs in coaching. But as with most people, I have had some bad times. My faith and staying true to the man God made me to be have helped me overcome the difficulties. I have also learned that difficult times present a wonderful opportunity to teach.

The number one goal of our program was to make our athletes better people. All decisions were based on that goal. That meant hiring coaches who believed the goal of any coach should be to make the team members not only better athletes but also better people. It meant running a program with character, a program that better prepared a young man who left us to be a husband, father, and contributing member of a community. This meant our first responsibility was to develop the complete person.

In the world of Division I football, winning with character is difficult. Many of the decisions I and my coaching staff made were not popular with the administration, fans, or media. Those decision, however, were crucial to building a program that not only won games but also changed lives.

One of the tasks I had the young men on my team undertake at the start of the year was to write down the things they valued. Inevitably, several kids' lists were dominated by things such as "be a starter this year," "lead the conference in rushing," or "compete for a national championship." I then shared my list with the team. On my list, family, faith in God, and being a person of character were always at the top. We then discussed what we valued and where it was truly important to place our priorities.

When a team sees that the coach values things beyond football, they can see there is more to life than the game. This is just one of countless opportunities we, as coaches, encounter to help make our athletes better people.

There are many ways to accomplish things as coaches, but knowing our people and motivating them is the most important aspect of success, in my opinion. During my coaching career, it was important for me not only to have the athletes identify their values but also to find out what motivated them. The only way to do this in a meaningful way was through personal contact and communication. Everyone is different, and everyone needs personal attention. I made it a point to spend time individually with each coach and athlete in my program. All athletes must be coached differently. To do this means getting to know them as people beyond what they can do on the field.

For the Team

While preparing for the 2003 football season, we felt we had a chance to be better than we had been in quite some time. We had finished the previous season with a bowl win over a talented University of Nebraska team from Lincoln. Still, the biggest hurdle facing us was that we were average in our own conference. Again, we had finished with four wins and four losses in the Southeastern Conference (SEC). This was a respectable record but not what we had been striving for. We had a senior quarterback, who was a great player, returning, along with quite a few talented upperclassmen.

We opened the season with a close win over our SEC opponent Vanderbilt University, of Nashville, Tennessee. Although we won, we certainly hadn't played well. The next two games, with the University of Memphis, from Tennessee, and Texas Tech of Lubbock, turned out to be disasters, as we played poorly and lost. I woke up the following Sunday morning with a record of one win and two losses — and a "for sale" sign in my yard. Someone else thought we had played as poorly as I thought we had.

The next game was on the road against a talented team from the University of Florida, in Gainesville. We had a record of one win and two losses as we headed to "the Swamp," the nickname for the Florida stadium. Everyone outside our team, from the fans to administration, was ready to panic and give up on the season. But teams are built on foundations of character and work ethic. We had a program that was about development. We had a group of seniors who had learned the right way to do things. Many of our seniors were from my first recruiting class, so they had been with the program for five years and had adopted as their own our team philosophy of character building and hard work. They never quit believing in each other or themselves. Through this character-building experience and great leadership from the staff, we found a way to beat Florida in the Swamp and go on to a seven-win, one-loss SEC record, a share of the SEC Western Division title, and a ten-win season. No one, except our team and coaches, expected the kind of success we achieved. This proved to me that we could build a program that produced young people of character and also produced wins. Winning will take care of itself if we prepare and build for it. It is a matter of staying with the program and not taking short cuts at the first signs of difficulty.

For the Individual Player

Being a person of character and working to develop well-rounded young people will present us with specific moments and youth who will stay with us forever. For example, when Peyton Manning did not win the Heisman Trophy in 1997, it was a difficult time for me, but it was also a great time to remember what is really important. It was a good time to remind Peyton of the difference between success and achievement. Success is merely someone else's view of what you are accomplishing—all-American honors, all-conference honors, Heisman Trophies. Achievment, though, is looking in the mirror and knowing you are the best man and the best player you can be. Achieving is a whole lot more important than success. For Peyton, not winning the Heisman was a great opportunity to find peace in the achievement of the man he had become.

When I first went to Ole Miss, we had a defensive end who had been playing hurt most of the season. When we came in as a new staff to prepare for the bowl game, I took him off the practice field and held him out of the game to give him time to heal. I required all injured athletes to travel and be with us at the bowl site. Since this defensive end was with us as part of the team, the same set of rules that applied to those playing in the game also applied to him. His behavior had been a constant challenge, with poor appearance, alcohol abuse, and tardiness. He was potentially a great player, but it was going to be a challenge to guide him to his potential. We began counseling and communicating that first winter. He was from a different region of the country and was struggling, being new to Mississippi. Communication was the key. We started guiding him through various life lessons. These lessons focused on aspects of his life off the field that would help him become the person God created him to be.

Once, we asked him to start focusing on others rather than himself. The assignment was simple. Wherever he happened to be, he was to exchange a greeting with everyone he encountered. One day, I received a call from the trainer's office, saying the staff there thought this player was up to something, because he had stopped by the past several days just to say hello. I had to smile, because I knew the lesson was taking hold. As time when on, he realized that we cared about him as a person, and he became a joy to work with. This young man went on to become one of the strongest team leaders I have ever known and now has a successful NFL career. He still conducts himself as a champion off the field. For this player, communication and feeling someone's sincere interest in him as a person, not only as an athlete, were the keys.

Final Thoughts

One of the joys of coaching for me is seeing the young men I have coached carry the values learned in a football program to their lives as husbands, fathers, and career men. They have learned that family and marriage require teamwork. A phrase we used with our team was "eleven people, one heartbeat." It signified that everyone was on the same page. Marriage and family are no different. The players have learned the importance of persevering and not quitting at the first adversity. Family life can be difficult, and we have to be willing to work through the difficulties when they arise. The players have also learned the benefits of hard work, be it in the family, in a relationship, or in the workplace. Many of the young men I coached have applied to their personal and professional lives the lessons of working hard and preparing adequately and have found these lessons instrumental to a successful life.

Coaching today requires us to wear many different hats. Players come to us for advice in all areas of life and, yes, even spirituality. When we are coaching more than one hundred young men, many events occur in their lives that require strength spiritually. Through the years, many have lost loved ones and are searching for comfort that can come only spiritually. I find that encouraging players to become active in the faith of their choice increases their ability to succeed on and off the field. Anyone who works with young people has this opportunity to present a spiritual message that can affect these young people the rest of their lives.

"Coach" is a special title I am proud to wear. For me, it means leading by example. It means being determined and committed to doing the right thing. It means recognizing that both failure and success are fleeting. The real challenge and joy is in the journey. It means focusing on helping young people develop the values that will serve them well in life and help them become the types of people they are proud of. It means helping them put first what is truly important in life. Most important, it means revealing to young people that the greatest success they can have in life is learning to live for others.

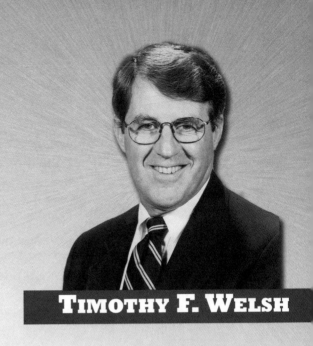

TIMOTHY F. WELSH

Tim Welsh has established himself as one of the most respected swimming coaches in the country over the course of his twenty-one-year tenure at the University of Notre Dame in South Bend, Indiana. Since arriving at Notre Dame in 1985, Tim has seen his teams post a dual-meet record of 252 wins and 141 losses (.641 percentage), while winning sixteen league titles (fifteen Midwestern Collegiate Conference [MCC] titles, one North Star title) and taking second place on five occasions (two MCC, three Big East). Before coaching at Notre Dame, Tim spent eight years as the head men's and women's coach at Johns Hopkins University, in Baltimore, Maryland. In 1978 and 1979, he led his teams to the NCAA Division III national championship.

Tim graduated magna cum laude from Providence College, in Providence, Rhode Island, in 1966. He went on to earn his master's degree at the University of Virginia, in Charlottesville, in 1967. Tim became the men's assistant coach at Syracuse University, in Syracuse, New York, in 1974 after leaving Winthrop College, in Rock Hill, South Carolina, where he taught English. During his four years at Syracuse, Tim continued to teach English, as well as designing and running the training program before joining the Johns Hopkins swimming program. Tim is an active member of the American Swimming Coaches

Association (ASCA), serving on its board of directors for the ninth time in 2005–2006 and was honored in 2004 with the association's prestigious Ousley Award for his distinguished service. Tim's student athletes have been traditionally strong in the classroom. Perennially on the Collegiate Swimming Coaches Association of America All-Academic list (which ranks teams according to grade point average [GPA]), his team claimed the top spot for GPA in the 1999 season and have been in the top ten eight times since 1990.

Tim and his wife, Jacqueline, are the parents of two sons, Tim and John. Tim, a 2002 Notre Dame graduate, participated in the university's Alliance for Catholic Education program before enrolling in an English PhD program at the University of Washington in Seattle. John is a 2005 Notre Dame graduate and is a graduate student in Italian at the University of Virginia.

CHAPTER 3

Developing the Whole Person Through Athletics and Coaching

Timothy F. Welsh

Coaches Are Teachers

Coaches are teachers. Coaches' students are the athletes on the team. The coaches' classrooms are the facilities where the athletes practice and compete. The athletes' formal subject matter is their sports, but their full subject matter is all of life. In the levels of athletics below professional sports, athletes are young people who are in the process of playing sports and growing up at the same time. Coaches at this level teach more than the X's and O's of their sports. They teach more than the playing of the game, and even more than the love of the game.

Somewhere, in all that playing of the game, something wonderful happens that makes athletics special. Amid all those practices and from all those competitions, athletes learn not only about the intricacies and beauties of the game, but they also learn about the intricacies and beauties of life. Most important, they learn about themselves. That learning is one of the things that makes athletics worthwhile. When people say that they "grew up playing sports," they are not kidding. They did grow up in the process of playing sports, and they discovered themselves while doing it.

Relationship

The catalyst for this transition from the games of sports to the game of life is frequently the coach. When athletics work as a transition, the bond between coaches and athletes is strong, powerful, and profound. The bond is based on trust, to begin with. Athletes put their faith in a coach as someone wiser, more knowledgeable, and more experienced in the sport and who is therefore able to guide them in the pursuit of athletic goals and achievement. The athletes agree to do what the coach asks and requires with full cooperation and full effort. The coach, in accepting the athletes' trust, agrees to take a personal interest in them. The coach agrees to care about the athletes as full human beings while athletes and coach go about learning and practicing the skills and strategies of their sport. Along the way, amid all the practices, all the exercises, all the effort, all the fatigue, all the exhilaration, all the frustration, all the success, all the competitions, all the travel, and all the time spent together, the transformation occurs. The athletes turn into more mature human beings, because the coach has turned into a mentor for the development of the athletes' characters.

The word *mentor* itself comes from Homer's classic poem the *Odyssey*. Mentor, a character in the poem, was a wise older man and a longtime friend of Ulysses, the main character. Mentor agreed to stay at home while Ulysses went off to fight in the Trojan War. Mentor's role at home was to look after Ulysses' son, Telemachus, and to give him good advice while his father was away. So important was Mentor's role as a trusted friend and adviser that, on occasion, Athena herself, a goddess of the ancient Greeks, descended from the heavens to inhabit Mentor's body to give the good advice that was needed. Dictionaries everywhere agree that the word *mentor* has since come to mean "a trusted counselor or guide."

The Catholic Church, with its interest in grounding both coaches and athletes in the Christian faith, offers a strong and supportive framework for this mentor-pupil relationship between coaches and athletes. In his first Mass with the athletic department at the University of Notre Dame in South Bend, Indiana, newly elected university president Fr. John I. Jenkins, a Holy Cross priest, emphasized this point in his homily by praising and thanking the athletic staff and coaches for their commitment to the whole culture and the whole lives of the student athletes at Notre Dame. He did not mention winning. From the University of Notre Dame in the world of collegiate athletics to the smallest Catholic school, coaches are encouraged and expected to teach in their practices and model in their lives the human values that lead to a life full of faith, good works, and ethical behavior. Coaches, in short, are called upon, and are expected, to be mentors for character development in their athletes.

Consistency and Team Culture

Both the simplest and the most powerful way this mentoring happens is through the coaches' consistency. When what the coaches teach matches how the coaches act; when how the coaches treat athletes is consistent with the way the coaches want to be treated by the athletes; when, to use an old-fashioned phrase, the coaches practice what they preach; or when, to use a more modern phrase, the coaches walk the talk; then, the message and the lessons the coaches teach and model are powerful and profound. These lessons are the ones the athletes learn and use not only in the sport but also in life. There is no substitute for this consistency. Coaches who are mentors all have it.

The foolproof test of whether the team has assimilated the values the coaches preach and teach is when those values become a part of the team's culture. Every team has a culture, or "the way we do things around here." The team culture is what teaches team members how to act in various circumstances. Team culture works. New team members want to know from the beginning "how things are done around here," and older team members take it upon themselves to teach the culture to the rookies. Unspoken team rules alone seldom define the team culture. Team behavior defines the team culture. Influencing the culture in a positive direction is one of the strongest areas in which coaches serve as mentors for their teams. The University of Notre Dame, for example, teaches and models for its students the value of doing community service work. As a result, community service projects are part of the team culture at Notre Dame. It is the way things are done around here.

On our men's swimming team, a dress code is a part of our culture. We dress up for travel and for major events. We do it because we are proud of our team and of our university, and we want to represent both of them well. So ingrained is this dress code in our team culture that our coaches seldom have to teach it anymore. The culture teaches it. We coaches just confirm that the culture is correct. In the years after they graduate, former swimmers often tell us with pride that they still use "dress code A" when they travel for their companies, even when they don't have to do so. We love hearing that. Our team culture has taught them the way we do things around here, and they still do it.

In Loco Parentis and Alma Mater

Schools sometimes refer to their role of trusted advisers as acting *in loco parentis.* This Latin phrase literally means acting "in the place of parents." Coaches, in most cases, are not the parents of the athletes they coach. Coaches should not try to be parents of their athletes, either. There is plenty of good folk wisdom on this topic for both coaches and parents—most of which reminds both of them that if they want to keep their own relationships with an athlete strong, they should stay out of the other's relationship with the athlete.

Nevertheless, even though coaches usually are not the athletes' parents, they are frequently called upon to act in the place of parents. Coaches act in the place of parents when they emphasize the morals, ethics, and character building associated with athletics. Values such as self-discipline, responsibility, honesty, fair play, teamwork, respect, courtesy, self-confidence, patience, hard work, reliability, concentration, and even understanding and forgiveness are all normal and natural parts of athletics. The best coaches, properly acting *in loco parentis,* teach all of them.

Athletics in a Catholic school embrace an *in loco parentis* philosophy. Coaches are expected to teach more than the rules of the game and physical fitness. They are expected to mentor and guide the moral, ethical, and personal development of their athletes. It is not enough in Catholic schools for athletes simply to play well or practice well. Their athletic performance is always coupled to their behavior. Play well, practice well—and live well. That is what is required, expected, and demanded in a Catholic school.

Catholic schools take another role seriously, too. It is the role of being an alma mater. In Latin, the word *alma* means "nourishing," and the word *mater* means "mother." A school that is our alma mater is a school that is our nourishing mother. Certainly, every nourishing mother wants what is best for her children, not just athletically and not just academically. A nourishing mother wants her children to grow and to develop as full and complete human beings who not only learn to become better players in the games of sports but also learn to become better players in the game of life. Once again, as it did by taking its role *in loco parentis* seriously, a Catholic school provides a holistic framework for a coach-athlete relationship by taking its role as an alma mater seriously.

When the next step is taken, from the "nourishing mother," who is our school, to the "Holy Mother," who is our Church, the values and the teaching that form the backdrop for a coach-athlete relationship become even more prominent. The emphasis in a Catholic school environment, from its most superficial to its most theological level, is always on the development of the whole person.

A Catholic School Is Different

The reason for all these extra requirements is both simple and profound. A Catholic school environment, by definition, is based on values. It is based on the theological, ethical, and moral teachings of the Catholic Church. It is an environment that seeks to emulate the teachings and example of the Gospels. It is an atmosphere based on respect, love, and forgiveness. Athletic performance in a Catholic school environment is still based on the same standards of athletic excellence that apply outside a Catholic school environment. Both coaches and athletes still do the same amount of work, with the same level of commitment and intensity. A win is still a win, a loss is still a loss, and a lifetime-best performance is still a lifetime-best performance. The difference is that within a Catholic school environment, athletic performance always has a religious context. So does coaching. So does the relationship between a coach and an athlete. The priorities and performances of athletes in a Catholic school are always measured by the standards of a Higher Authority. In a Catholic school, when a conflict occurs between what appear to be purely athletic priorities and the standards demanded by the Higher Authority, coaches themselves are expected to follow the standards of the Higher Authority and to teach their athletes to follow those standards, too. It is part of their role as mentors for character development.

When a coach and an athlete are together in a Catholic school environment, the importance and significance of their relationship deepens and intensifies. In a Catholic school, a connection to the spiritual world is always present. Nurturing the spirit is always supported, and pathways between the athletic world and the spiritual one are consciously sought. A peak performance in athletics, as many an elite athlete will testify, often has a strong spiritual component to it.

A Deeper Look

Two more parts remain in this discussion of the role of coaches as mentors for athletes in character development. The first part is to look at coaches themselves to see what they might believe and demonstrate to influence their athletes. The second is to look at athletes and their experiences to see what about being an athlete allows coaches to influence so profoundly the development of athletes' characters.

What Coaches Believe

Coaches are optimists. Whatever their personal tendencies might be to find fault or be critical, coaches are still optimists. Coaches believe in change. They believe in growth. They believe that people, certainly the people on their own teams, can learn and get better. They believe that skills can be taught, learned, and repeated appropriately in athletic competition. They believe that with enough practice, preparation, and self-discipline, a set of athletic tasks can be done right. They believe that when enough athletic tasks are done right, a game can be played well. They also believe that no matter how well a game is played today, it can always be played better the next time. So, while coaches believe in improvement, they do not believe in perfection. There is always something to work on and to improve.

So what do coaches and athletes do on the day after a game? They go right back to practice. They go right back to working on their game, always with the hope, the intention, and the desire to do even better the next time. At major swimming competitions, for example, it is common to see the swimmer who set a world or American record yesterday back in the pool today, working with a coach on fundamental drills and skills in preparation for the next race. There is a rhythm to the process—first the performance, then acceptance of and taking responsibility for the outcome, followed by reviewing and setting new goals, and finally the self-discipline of going back to do the practice that leads to the improvement that leads to the next great performance. Coaches and athletes go through this process together. The role of the coaches is to be the guides. The role of the athletes is to allow themselves to be guided. The process always begins with trust, and it always ends with taking responsibility for one's own actions. In the middle is hard work and self-discipline.

Seeing the character development and human value in this lifestyle takes little imagination. Just imagine what life might be like if every workplace, for example, were filled with workers and supervisors who were living this athletic lifestyle. Every effort would be a full effort. Workers would take responsibility for every one of their actions. Supervisors would point out ways to continue to improve and would teach the workers the skills required to make the improvement. Every success would be followed by a humble return to fundamentals and a commitment to do even better the next time. Clearly, athletes who learn these values and habits from their coaches learn life skills that are rare, useful, and extremely helpful in the real world.

The process coaches and athletes go through to continue improving in their sports applies not only to the athletic world but also to the spiritual one. In short, it is simply good theology. It is good theology to believe that people can change and improve. It is good theology to have hope and be optimistic. It is good theology to believe that mistakes can be corrected, that good habits can be learned, and that a person's actions can become better than they are now. It is good theology to take responsibility for one's own actions, to be humble in the face of one's errors, and to make a firm commitment not to repeat those mistakes the next time. Finally, it is good theology to recognize that one needs a guide and a model to learn how to perform consistently on a higher level. The athletic world and the spiritual world are often closer together than one might suspect. In a Catholic school environment, it is possible for both the coach and the athlete to live in both worlds. It is also possible for both of them to use what they learn in one realm to help make sense of and understand the other.

The Athletes and Their Experiences

Young athletes, particularly those in middle school and high school, frequently know more about their sports and more about themselves in their sports than they know about anything else. Learning to apply what they know about themselves in their sports to what they want to know about themselves in other areas of life is a skill that leads to significant self-knowledge, maturity, and character development.

An area as simple as preparing for and taking a test in school is a perfect example of this. Athletes know how to prepare for major competitions. They learn in their sports how to work, rest, eat, sleep, and focus for major athletic events. They also learn in their sports what to do if they don't do as well in competition as they had hoped. They know whom to ask about their mistakes. They know what to work on. They even work on it without being reminded. No athlete would think of starting to train on the night before a big game, but the same athlete, in the role of student, may start to study on the night before a big test. No athlete would expect to play well in a game if she or he stayed up the night before, but the same student may expect to do well on a final exam by pulling an all-nighter studying. No athlete who played a game poorly would think of going back to practice without trying to correct his or her mistakes, but the same student may get back a test paper and not go back to restudy the areas where most of the mistakes occurred. No athlete who loafs and doesn't pay attention in practice expects to do well in the game, but the same student who loafs and doesn't pay attention in class may indeed expect to get a good grade in the course. Athletes clearly have a lot to learn by crossing over their skills from one discipline to another. Here, too, coaches can serve as effective and helpful mentors to their athletes. They can encourage, teach, coach, and support them as they practice becoming as well organized, as well prepared, and as coachable academically as they are athletically.

Why Athletics?

A final question remains for this discussion: Why athletics? What makes athletics such a rich and fertile field for character development? What makes coaches such strong and influential mentors? Why toil in this field of athletics and character development? An answer lies in the nature of athletics themselves and in the nature of athletic preparation.

It's Only a Game

Athletics, first of all, are games. Games should be, and often are, played for the fun of them. Even professional athletics on TV are considered entertainment. One characteristic of athletics that allows them to be so important in the lives of athletes is that, on the scale of ultimate values, athletics are not very important. The athletic world is a safe place to commit oneself and to take risks to learn about oneself, because ultimately, it is not an important world. An athlete can put 100 percent effort into an athletic endeavor and lose (or not have things work out as hoped), and life is still okay. An imperfectly played game may be a loss, and all the effort put into the preparation may not have worked out well, but life goes on, and another game can be prepared for and played another day. Everyone knows this. Coaches even teach it: "It's only a game."

Compare the safety of that position to the theological dangers inherent in the real world. Although, on the one hand, an imperfectly played game can be replayed or forgotten, an imperfectly lived life, on the other hand, cannot. What is there to lose with an imperfectly lived life? Everything. Real life is too serious to be played with. The stakes are too high. The constant testing of limits and resetting of goals, the constant push to go to the edge of failure and return that characterize athletic training and competition are too risky for real-world activities. The best coaches of young people understand this, and that is why they give their heart and soul to athletics. In essence, when coaches commit themselves to the development of the whole person, not just the athlete, they are letting the athlete take risks and make mistakes in the safe world of sports rather than the real world. They teach athletes character development where it is safe, where mistakes are correctable, and where there is always one more game to prepare for. Coaches let the learning take place in this semiartificial world, with its rules, boundaries, beginnings, endings, time-outs, halftimes, and clear decisions, even bad ones. Giving 100 percent is safe here. Even failing is safe here. No one's life depends on it. Nothing that happens here lives in eternity. The athletic world may have its winners and losers, and American society does take those terms seriously, but the real world has saints and sinners. Better to end the game as a loser than to end life as a sinner.

Coaching Is More

Athletics are fertile grounds for character development, because of the nature of athletic preparation and the nature of the relationship between athletes and coaches. Because the whole person competes in an athletic event, and because, therefore, the whole person must be trained for athletic performance, everything in the coach-athlete relationship is relevant to athletic performance. Coaches are, and must be, interested in every aspect of an athlete's life.

Compare a coach's interest in an athlete, for example, with an academic teacher's interest in a student. For the coach, everything that relates to the whole person is related to athletic performance, so the coach will want to know and pay attention to everything, including an athlete's eating and sleeping habits; general state of health and fitness level; relationships with parents, friends, girlfriends, boyfriends, or other players on the team; recent practice history; temptations to drink, smoke, use other drugs, gamble, cheat, and so forth. None of those factors even begins to touch on athletic ability, but they are relevant to both the coach and the athlete. An academic teacher, on the other hand, is far more limited in what information is relevant to the classroom, and even in what is permissible to know. As if that were not enough of a difference, a student's English teacher may change every year or every semester, but an athlete's coach is likely to remain constant for several years. Coaches must know the athlete this well, to do their jobs well. Coaching, from this perspective becomes a high form of teaching, because it is a complete form of teaching.

Coaches and athletes together typically work through athletic and academic issues. Academic teachers are typically limited to their subject matter. When it comes to counting hours, coaches typically spend more time per week and per year with their athletes than do any other adult role models in the athletes' lives. By the time the athletes are in high school or are involved in year-round training, this role model comparison even includes the athletes' parents. If the athletes have driver's licenses and drive themselves to practice or school, the time spent with parents falls far below the time spent with coaches.

The conclusion is inescapable. Coaches are influential in the lives of athletes because they often know the athletes better than do any other adults. Coaches become mentors for character development in athletes because they are there and care and are involved when the athletes' characters develop. These are large factors.

Something Wonderful

In an even more active role, coaches become mentors for character development in their athletes, because their teaching and training lead the athletes directly to the major breakthrough performances and discoveries of their athletic lives. Student athletes typically are too young to experience genuine human excellence in other areas of their lives. It is possible for them to experience genuine human excellence in athletics. Here again, the coaches typically point the way and select the path that leads to this excellence. No matter the level of excellence athletes achieve, however, the method of training and preparation follows a similar pattern. Athletes must always push past their old limits to reach new ones. This process of pushing past old limits and reaching new ones is a continual process of self-discovery, all led, guided, and directed by coaches.

Something wonderful happens between coaches and athletes that begins in athletic performance and then leads far beyond it into the realm of human growth, character development, joy, and even beauty. Catholic theologians might call it the work of the Holy Spirit, and so it might be. Whatever it is, the spirit of this mentor-athlete relationship is real and powerful and is one of the principal glories of the coaching world.

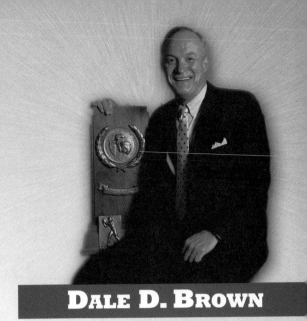

DALE D. BROWN

Dale Brown began his coaching career as a high school coach in North Dakota, where he coached basketball, wrestling, football, and track and field. He was an assistant coach at Utah State University in Logan for five years and for one year at Washington State University in Seattle, before becoming the head coach at Louisiana State University (LSU) in Baton Rouge in 1972. He is the winningest coach in LSU basketball history. He also is the second winningest coach in SEC history. Of 160 of Dale's players, 104 received their college degrees, and those who attended LSU for four years had a graduation rate of 84 percent.

While attending Minot State University in North Dakota, Dale earned twelve letters in basketball, football, and track. In 1957, he received a BS degree from Minot State and in 1964, he received an MS degree from the University of Oregon, in Eugene. Dale is a member of the North Dakota and Louisiana Sports Halls of Fame and of the North Dakota and Louisiana Basketball Coaches Halls of Fame. Dale now resides in Baton Rouge, Louisiana, serves as an analyst for Fox Sports Radio, and is an author and motivational speaker.

CHAPTER 4

Helping Athletes Clear the Four Hurdles

Dale D. Brown

Early Influences

My Mom's Effect on Me

I guess you could say that my story of faith started two days before I was born. Two days before I was born, my so-called father — I've always referred to him as "my mother's husband" — left my mother, two young sisters, eleven and twelve years of age, and me, and he never returned. His departure put my mother in a difficult position. She had an eighth-grade education, came off the farm in North Dakota, and couldn't get a job during the Great Depression in 1935. In the cold prairies of North Dakota, she had to do two things that were very unpleasant for her: she became a baby-sitter to earn money, and she had to put our family on welfare. We lived in a one-room apartment above a bar and hardware store, and I remember my mother getting $42.50 in Ward County welfare each month. She sat down and meticulously decided what breads and canned goods we could buy for the coming week.

Twice during these difficult times, my mother taught me a lesson that has stayed with me during my whole coaching career. Two times, I saw my mother get on her winter coat, walk down a flight of stairs, and take back to the Red Owl and the Piggly Wiggly grocery stores 25 cents and 40 cents, because the clerks had given her too much change for the groceries she'd brought home. Seeing her dressing in the middle of winter, I said, "Mama, where are you going?" She said, "Oh, I'm taking this money back to the store. They gave me too much change." It reminds me of an anonymous poem written years ago that said:

I'd rather see a lesson than hear one any day.
I'd rather you walk with me than to merely show the way.
The eye is a better teacher, and more willing than the ear.
And counsel is confusing but example's always clear.
The best of all the teachers are the ones who live the creed.
To see good put into action is what everybody needs.
I soon can learn to do it if you let me see it done.
I can see your hand in action, but your tongue too fast may run.
And the counsel you are giving may be very fine and true,
but I'd rather get my lessons by observing what you do.

I observed immediately a basic character in my mother that has stayed with me my whole life — that is, to be honest.

I saw other lessons in the life of this woman who had no PhD behind her name. Not once, after being abandoned, did I hear my mother talk negatively about the man who had walked out on us and never returned, never sent any money, never wrote. She didn't drink, and she never smoked. I never heard her swear. She was never bitter.

My mother's Catholic faith was unbelievable. She brought us to Mass and Communion daily — not just Sunday, but daily. For me, the daily trip to church was a ritual. To my numerous fake illnesses and attempts to avoid going, my mom's response was always, "Get up, Son. We're going to Mass and Communion." The spirit that grew in that little, one-room apartment we lived in, uncomfortable and cramped though it was, made it attractive.

Being a small place, the apartment never provided any place for us to get away on our own. So at night, I often went to sit above the alley on the fire escape. One night, the faith my mother instilled in me deepened when I came back in from sitting out there. My mom asked me to sit in her little rocker. She pulled up the footstool and said, "Son, I notice you go outside at night a lot. What do you think about when you're out there, sitting on that fire escape?" I didn't have to ponder the answer. I said, "Mama, I think of three things. I think of travel." (We didn't own a car, a bicycle, or any other form of transportation.) "I think of mountains." (North Dakota is a very flat state, flatter than the top of a table.) "And I think about learning—I want to learn as much as I can."

My mother hesitated just a moment and then said, "You know, Son, I'm going to tell you something. I'm embarrassed to tell you this, but I need to teach you a lesson. You know when these people come to pick me up to go baby-sit? I'm so embarrassed. There's no husband in our house. We live in this little one-room apartment. I've just got an eighth-grade education. My clothes smell of mothballs." (She bought her clothes at rummage sales.) "So I'm so worried about my image when these big shots come to pick me up. I look up big words in the dictionary, and then all the way to their house," she said, "I inject these big words into conversation to try to distract them. That's called making an image. When you sit out there on the fire escape at night, just you and God, that's your true character. And Son," she said, "if you spend too much time polishing your image, you'll eventually tarnish your character and be an unhappy man." That night, my mom taught me that being my true self—as when I was on the fire escape—was more important than trying to impress people with my image or with who I thought they wanted me to be.

The Church's Effect on Me

No matter how financially tight things got around the house, Mom always scraped together enough money for me to attend Catholic school. I learned a great deal over the course of the twelve years I was in Catholic school. I learned that rules were important. I learned we all are on this earth to help each other.

Two particular lessons I learned stand out profoundly in my mind. One morning, I was standing with two friends by the radiators in the hall at school, warming up. We had religion class before school every day at 8:00 a.m., and we were out there before class, talking about the things kids talk about. One of the guys said, "Yeah, the Salvation Army, isn't that funny what they do? You know, they're outside ringing the bell, and they've got that little pot." Not really making fun of the Salvation Army, but sort of jesting, like kids do. Well, the bell rang, so we went to religion class. Our religion teacher was Father Hogan. He called on the three of us who had been talking in the hall and asked us to stand up. He said, "You know, I heard you three boys out there talking about the Salvation Army. I wonder, do any of you guys know the motto of the Salvation Army?"

We each responded, "No, Father."

Father Hogan continued, "Well, let me tell you what it is. It's to love those who aren't loved by anyone else. The next time you good Catholics are going to make fun of something, remember that." To this day, that lesson about compassion and sensitivity has stayed with me. Every year at Christmas, when I'm shopping with my wife or daughter and we encounter a Salvation Army volunteer with a red kettle and ringing bell, I walk over and put money in the pot. I also share with that volunteer what that wonderful priest taught me.

Father Hogan taught me a second lesson, on the importance of being prompt. There are rules. And rules are not to be bent, twisted, manipulated, or bartered with. The moment I learned this lesson is vivid in my mind. The sports teams at our tiny Catholic school played the biggest schools in the state. We had just a hundred kids in our whole high school. I thought I was a big shot athlete. I broke all the records in the history of North Dakota basketball and was the leading scorer in the history of this little school. I led the state in scoring, I had just come off being class president. I was on the homecoming court. I broke the school record in the quarter mile race. I was a star on the football team—and I thought I was something! Getting a little full of myself, I felt some of the rules didn't necessarily apply to me.

Every Monday afternoon by 1:00, we had to turn in an eligibility slip to play sports that week. One Monday afternoon, I took my eligibility slip down to the office and laid it on the desk of Father Hogan, who by then was the principal of the school. Holding my eligibility slip in one hand, he looked over the top of his horn-rimmed glasses at the clock on the wall. "Dale," he said, "what time does that clock on my wall say?"

I had no idea where he was headed, so I said, "One-fifteen."

He held my eligibility slip in front of my face and he said, "What time was this due?"

I said, "One o'clock."

"Ah-hah, that's good you can tell time, and that you know when it was due." He started ripping my eligibility slip into small pieces. Then he deposited the pieces in the wastebasket and said, "Now get back up in the room and start learning promptness. This slip was due at one o'clock. You're not going on the road trip this week." I thought he must be joking. After all, I was the superstar of the school. Well, guess who didn't go on the road trip!

What Athletics Have Taught Me

Athletics gave me my first good self-image. I had a terrible inferiority complex, coming from a home with no father and surviving on welfare. Athletics helped me begin to see myself in a different light, as a person who is more than the circumstances into which I was born. From athletics, I also learned what true discipline meant. I learned teamwork. I learned respect for others. All these lessons gave me the opportunity to obtain a scholarship to go to college and get a higher education.

Athletics also allowed me to meet the man whom many consider the greatest coach ever to have lived and the finest man I've ever met, former UCLA men's basketball coach John Wooden. Coach Wooden taught me the truth about success. He said, "Success is peace of mind, which is a direct result of self-satisfaction in knowing you made the effort in becoming the best that you are capable of becoming." Of all the things I've learned in my life, this is one lesson I truly strive to teach the athletes I coach to help them prepare not only for sports but also for life beyond sports.

Four Hurdles

I used to share with my athletes my belief that we live in a world of paradoxes and that these paradoxes create many of the problems we encounter. For example, we've multiplied our possessions but reduced our values. We have more college degrees but less common sense. We've conquered outer space but can't seem to conquer inner space. We've learned how to make a living but not a life. We've added years to life but not life to years.

So what can we do? To find happiness and success, we all must learn to negotiate four hurdles. These are things we can't con, cheat, barter, buy, or lie our way over. Instead, we have to meet them head on. All of us can get over these hurdles if we have commitment and the discipline to do it. Commitment and discipline are the spinal cord of true success. Until one is committed, there is hesitation. When our focus changes, our life will change.

It's difficult to get over these four hurdles, because there are so many temptations that might distract us—the temptation to take the shortcut, to cheat, to manipulate, to maneuver, to not work hard. But when we face and overcome these four hurdles, we can achieve true success and find happiness.

Hurdle One: "I Can't"

We don't even scratch the surface of our greatness. Whatever your mind can conceive and believe, it can do with commitment and perseverance. If we did all the things we are capable of doing, we would astonish ourselves. It is easier, however, to make excuses about why we can't do something or to blame others for making our success impossible. Once you blame others, you've given up the power to change. It's easier to say, "I can't," so we have to learn to overcome that.

When we stop making excuses or looking to place blame, we can achieve amazing things. For example, Walt Disney was advised to pursue another line of work, because he'd never be a successful cartoonist or movie producer. Albert Einstein's teacher told him he was not smart enough to pursue a scientific education. And then there is a young man I coached, Shaquille O'Neal. He told me once at my summer camp, "People always used to tell me, 'You're not going to be anything.' But I never gave up." He was cut from his high school basketball team. His high school coach told him he was too slow and too clumsy, had too big feet, and could never be a successful basketball player.

These people, and countless other examples, had a belief system in them that they could do it. They were able to overcome hurdle number one and go on to do spectacular things. A poem written years ago says:

If you think you are beaten, you are.
If you think you dare not, you don't.
If you like to win, but think you can't,
It is almost certain you won't.
If you think you'll lose, you're lost,
For out in the world we find,
Success begins with a fellow's will.
It's all in the state of mind.

If you think you are outclassed, you are.
You've got to think high to rise,
You've got to be sure of yourself before
You can ever win a prize.

Life's battles don't always go
To the stronger or faster man.
But soon or late, the man who wins,
Is the man who thinks he can.

(C. W. Longenecker)

Hurdle Two: Overcoming Failure and Guilt

The second hurdle we have to overcome is being afraid to fail. Success often is built on multiple failures. Until we learn to derive lessons from our failures, we'll keep repeating those failures and keep digging ourselves into a deeper hole. The secret to success is in rising every time you fall and in never giving up.

History provides us numerous examples of highly successful people who confronted many, and major, failures but who still made their dreams come true. Failure's only a detour, and an opportunity to begin again. The most successful people I know, in almost every profession, have not been afraid to fail. When they have fallen down, they get back up.

In July 1954, Martin Luther King Jr. gave a wonderful speech called "What Is Man?" He said, "We know that man is made for the stars, created for the everlasting, and born for eternity. We know that man's crowned with glory and honor. But so long as he lives on the low level, he'll be frustrated, disillusioned, and bewildered." Every time I lived on that low level, I was frustrated, disillusioned, and bewildered. The famous American writer Henry David Thoreau hit the nail on the head when he said, "What lies behind us and what lies ahead of us are tiny matters compared to what lives within us." So we've got to quit worrying. It doesn't do any good. We've got to replace worry with positive action. We shouldn't be afraid. We can do it.

Every day we walk this earth, our courage will be tested in some way. But if we approach life one day at a time, we won't break down. There are two days we shouldn't worry about—yesterday and tomorrow. When we live in those two eternities, we lose what is today and will not be ready to face the challenges it brings.

Hurdle Three: Handicaps

Hurdle number three is our handicaps. Quite simply, a handicap is a disadvantage that makes achievement difficult. We all have handicaps of some sort, whether we recognize them or not. To succeed, we have to confront our handicaps and overcome them. You can learn a great deal about yourself when you are staring your handicap in the eye. You have the choice to respond by accepting your handicap as final and then giving up, or by accepting your handicap as another challenge to overcome and then fighting to achieve in spite of it.

A man recently won the Tour de France bicycle race for the seventh straight time—an unprecedented achievement. Seven times in a row, Lance Armstrong has worn the race leader's famed yellow jersey on the last day's ride through Paris down the Champs Elysees. Before his first victory, however, he encountered a major life hurdle. In 1996, Lance was diagnosed with testicular cancer, abdominal cancer, and numerous tumors in his lung and brain. Lance did not use his illness as an excuse. Instead, early in the treatment, he began referring to himself as a cancer survivor rather than a cancer victim. In 2005, seven Tour de France victories under his belt, Lance proved the result of not conceding to a handicap. Through the LIVESTRONG Foundation, which he founded, Lance continues to help others become cancer survivors rather than victims.

A friend of mine, Paul Anderson, was diagnosed with Bright's disease at the age of five. Bright's disease affects the kidney and causes lifelong health issues. It can be fatal in some cases. Paul refused to accept the limitations of his condition. He worked every day to build himself up and become as strong as he could. He began to weightlift competitively and went on to win the U.S. National Amateur Athletic Union Weightlifting Championship and the gold medal in the super heavyweight division in the 1956 summer Olympics. He also broke nine weightlifting world records. He was commonly called "the strongest man in the world."

When I was a high school coach in North Dakota, I read that Paul was going to appear at a Fellowship of Christian Athletes (FCA) camp in Estes Park, Colorado. I said, "I'm driving there. I've got to see this world record holder. I've got to see this unbelievable human being." I wanted to know what made him do it and how he did it. I drove to Estes Park and sat in the front row of nine hundred other people in the arena. He walked onto the stage, not saying a word. Onstage were sawhorses and a two-by-four board lying across them. Paul stepped back, took a ten-penny nail from a nearby podium, took a handkerchief, which he held in his hand, stepped back, and with one thrust of his hand, drove the nail right through the two-by-four. Then he looked at the audience, and this was his entire speech: "Good morning, everybody. My name is Paul Anderson. I am the strongest man in the history of the world. And I cannot live one day without God." He turned and walked off the stage. I learned that day that I can't live one day without God, either. Powerful and strong though we think we are, when we learn this wonderful lesson, as Paul did, we can overcome any handicap.

Hurdle Four: Knowing Yourself

The fourth and final hurdle is the struggle to know yourself. This is the hardest one for us all. Who am I? Where am I going? What do I want from life? People are one of three things: what they think they are, what others think they are, and what they really are. When we really know ourselves, we begin to develop. Real confidence comes from knowing and accepting ourselves, knowing our strengths and limitations, as opposed to depending upon affirmation from others. The beginning of wisdom is being honest with ourselves.

The most noble and perfect victory is the triumph over one's self. Muhammad Ali, maybe the greatest boxer of all time, commented that he had achieved complete success by the world's standards, but that success had not brought him true happiness. He concluded that the only sure way for people to be happy was to be honest with themselves and give their lives to God.

"Pistol Pete" Maravich, whom I consider the greatest college basketball player ever, averaged forty-four points a game. He had everything in the world, but he said all of it—the money, fame, and other things—left him empty. Only when he totally submitted and gave his life to God did he find true happiness and peace. You see, when Muhammad Ali and Pistol Pete changed their attitudes, their lives changed, and they found true success and happiness. For these men, and for us, as well, knowing ourselves means recognizing our dependence on God. Knowing ourselves means being able to say with confidence, "I can, and I deserve to, find happiness and success because I'm made in the image of God. So under no circumstances will I ever lose hope or give up, no matter what my failures are."

Being a Leader

If there were ever a moment in our history when leadership was needed, it is now. With all the evil, all the temptations, and all the bad things going on in the world, we need leaders. A common quality of great leaders through the ages has been their mastery at articulating a vision of the future. They see something that is not yet there and can relay the image to others. In any leadership position, the most important aspect of the job is getting everyone to work together.

However, working together is only a beginning. The world needs leaders who find their strength in faith and character. As coaches, we hold a special role as leaders of young people. Our roles as exceptional leaders will get our team members to feel they're an integral part of a common goal. How do we do this? This may sound odd, but the underlying theme of teamwork is our ability to convey a renewed sense of optimism. Teamwork doesn't just happen—it takes a captain to steer it in the right direction. Our role as the captain—whether we're a coach, a teacher, a father, a mother, or whatever—is to give the ship direction, purpose, and ultimately, success. I read a saying years ago: "The role of most leaders is to get the people to think more of the leader. But the role of the exceptional leader is to get the people to think more of themselves."

We need to make a difference, but we can do it only through the grace of God. I am convinced that we are capable of solving any problem, whether of race, crime, pollution, drugs, or whatever plagues humanity.

You, with God's help, are responsible for your future. You're really free the moment you don't look outside yourself for someone to solve your problems. You will know that you're free when you no longer blame anyone or anything but realize you control your destiny and are capable of changing the world. People can be divided into three groups: those who make things happen, those who watch things happen, and those who wonder what happened. We've got to decide which group we will be in.

In conclusion, the most important thing to God is our relationships with one another. God made us in such a way that everybody needs somebody. And God's idea for success is a community, a group of people who are committed to each other and who strive to follow his will. Communities and nations will be transformed when humanity returns to God and his purposes. Humans have not advanced a centimeter in the history of the world by fighting, hating, killing, and competing. The only notable advancement humans have ever made is becoming brothers and sisters who labor toward a common goal. You see, the best potential of "me" is "we." So the question in our life journey over the four hurdles is not whether God can bring peace, love, and happiness in the world. The question is, can we?

ACKNOWLEDGMENTS

The scriptural quotations contained herein are from the New Revised Standard Version of the Bible, Catholic Edition. Copyright © 1993 and 1989 by the Division of Christian Education of the National Council of the Churches of Christ in the United States of America. All rights reserved.

The excerpt on page 8 is from *Take Time for Paradise: Americans and Their Games,* by A. Bartlett Giamatti (New York: Simon and Schuster, 1989), page 15. Copyright © 1989 by the Estate of A. Bartlett Giamatti.

The quotation by Coach John Wooden on page 55 is from Coach John Wooden's Official Web site, *www.coachjohnwooden.com/pyramidofsuccess.html,* accessed February 25, 2006.

The poem by C. W. Longenecker on pages 56–57 is from Cybernation. Com, *www.cybernation.com/victory/youcandoit/youcan.php,* accessed February 25, 2006.

The quotation by Martin Luther King Jr. on page 57 is from the Men's Day sermon at Dexter Avenue Baptist Church in Montgomery, Alabama, July 11, 1954.

The quotation by Henry David Thoreau on pages 57–58 is from BrainyQuote, *www.brainyquote.com/quotes/quotes/h/henrydavid145971. html,* accessed February 25, 2006.

To view copyright terms and conditions for Internet materials cited here, log on to the home pages for the referenced Web sites.

During this book's preparation, all citations, facts, figures, names, addresses, telephone numbers, Internet URLs, and other pieces of information cited within were verified for accuracy. The authors and Saint Mary's Press staff have made every attempt to reference current and valid sources, but we cannot guarantee the content of any source, and we are not responsible for any changes that may have occurred since our verification. If you find an error in, or have a question or concern about, any of the information or sources listed within, please contact Saint Mary's Press.